3/18

COMING TOGETHER TO CELEBRATE

GROUNDHOG DAY

Katie Gillespie

LET'S READ
AV2 BY WEIGL™
ADDED VALUE • AUDIO VISUAL

www.av2books.com

LET'S READ AV²
BY WEIGL™
ADDED VALUE • AUDIO VISUAL

AV² provides enriched content that supplements and complements this book. Weigl's AV² books strive to create inspired learning and engage young minds in a total learning experience.

Your AV² Media Enhanced books come alive with...

Audio
Listen to sections of the book read aloud.

Video
Watch informative video clips.

Embedded Weblinks
Gain additional information for research.

Try This!
Complete activities and hands-on experiments.

Key Words
Study vocabulary, and complete a matching word activity.

Quizzes
Test your knowledge.

Slide Show
View images and captions, and prepare a presentation.

... and much, much more!

Go to www.av2books.com, and enter this book's unique code.

BOOK CODE

H696989

AV² by Weigl brings you media enhanced books that support active learning.

Published by AV² by Weigl
350 5th Avenue, 59th Floor
New York, NY 10118

Website: www.av2books.com

Copyright ©2018 AV² by Weigl

Library of Congress Control Number: 2017930490

ISBN 978-1-4896-5911-8 (hardcover)
ISBN 978-1-4896-5912-5 (softcover)
ISBN 978-1-4896-5913-2 (multi-user eBook)

Printed in the United States of America in Brainerd, Minnesota
1 2 3 4 5 6 7 8 9 0   21 20 19 18 17

022017
020317

Editor: Katie Gillespie   Designer: Ana María Vidal

Weigl acknowledges Getty Images, iStock, Alamy, and Newscom as the primary image suppliers for this title.

CONTENTS

Groundhog Day is celebrated on February 2 every year.

It is a day to find out how long winter will last.

Groundhog Day has been celebrated in America for 130 years. It is named after a furry animal that lives in a hole under the ground.

The groundhog comes out of its hole on Groundhog Day.
It is said that spring will come early if the groundhog does not see its shadow.

People say there will be **six more weeks of winter** if the groundhog **sees its shadow**.

Groundhog Day comes from a tradition called Candlemas. Settlers from Germany brought it to Pennsylvania in the 1700s.

The **first** American **Groundhog Day celebration** took place on **February 2, 1887**.

People come together on Groundhog Day.

The largest celebration is held at Gobbler's Knob in Punxsutawney, Pennsylvania.

One way to celebrate Groundhog Day is to watch the groundhog ceremony. Some people go in person. Others watch on television.

The **2001** Punxsutawney ceremony was shown **live** in Times Square, **New York City**.

Groundhog Day is also celebrated in other places across the United States.

Events take place each year in Lincoln, Massachusetts and Garner, North Carolina.

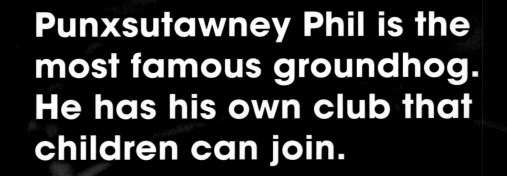

Punxsutawney Phil is the most famous groundhog. He has his own club that children can join.

Groundhog Day events in Punxsutawney last all week long. There are fireworks, concerts, tours, and other fun activities.

Tens of thousands of people come to Punxsutawney to **celebrate** each year.

GROUNDHOG DAY FACTS

This page provides more details about the interesting facts found in the book. They are intended to be used by adults as a learning support to help young readers round out their knowledge of each celebration featured in the *Coming Together to Celebrate* series.

Pages 4–5

Groundhog Day is celebrated on February 2 every year. In the Northern Hemisphere, winter begins around December 21 or 22. This is called the winter solstice. It is the shortest day of the year, when the Sun moves the shortest distance in the sky. Winter lasts for three months until the vernal equinox, when the season officially changes. However, warmer temperatures can make it feel like spring has come early.

Pages 6–7

Groundhog Day has been celebrated in America for 130 years. Groundhogs are also called woodchucks. They are part of the squirrel family. Groundhogs have coarse gray or brown fur. They eat grass, leaves, fruit, and tree bark, but do not need to drink very much water. It is important for groundhogs to eat a lot in the summer and fall so that they can build up enough fat to last through the winter.

Pages 8–9

The groundhog comes out of its hole on Groundhog Day. Groundhogs hibernate in the winter. While in this state, they slow down their breathing and heart rate, and lower their body temperature. Groundhogs stay in underground holes called burrows while hibernating. A groundhog's burrow is usually found under farmland or open meadows. Burrows can be up to 66 feet (20 meters) in length.

Pages 10–11

Groundhog Day comes from a tradition called Candlemas. It is a festival to honor the day Jesus Christ was presented to God by the Virgin Mary. In the Middle Ages, people thought animals such as the badger would come out of hibernation for Candlemas. If it was sunny, the animal would see its shadow, signifying six more weeks of winter. When German settlers brought the legend to America, the badger became a groundhog.

People come together on Groundhog Day. Gobbler's Knob is known as the "Weather Capital of the World." Each February 2, people gather there to watch the groundhog ceremony. There is one viewing area for students and one for families. Bonfires keep everyone warm from the time the gate opens at 3:00 AM until the groundhog emerges to make its prediction at 7:25 AM.

One way to celebrate Groundhog Day is to watch the groundhog ceremony. The 2001 ceremony was broadcast on the Times Square JumboTron. The groundhog saw his shadow when he was placed on the maple stump. He predicted that there would be six more weeks of winter.

Groundhog Day is also celebrated in other places across the United States. Ms. G is the Massachusetts State Groundhog. She lives at Drumlin Farm in Lincoln, where people gather for her yearly weather predictions. Ms. G has her own children's book. In addition to a groundhog named Snerd, people can see birds and other animals at the celebrations in Garner, North Carolina.

Punxsutawney Phil is the most famous groundhog. He is also the official groundhog of Groundhog Day. Punxsutawney Phil lives at the Gobbler's Knob town library. He was named after British King Phillip. Children ages 12 and under can join the Jr. Groundhog Club. Members receive an official membership card and certificate, as well as a monthly activity newsletter.

Groundhog Day events in Punxsutawney last all week long. Activities range from hay ride historical tours to groundhog cookie decorating. Fans can even join Punxsutawney Phil for breakfast at Gobbler's Knob or spend time with him at the Groundhog Ball masquerade. Other fun events include scavenger hunts, a top hat decorating contest, and the Groundhog Day Dance.

KEY WORDS

Research has shown that as much as 65 percent of all written material published in English is made up of 300 words. These 300 words cannot be taught using pictures or learned by sounding them out. They must be recognized by sight. This book contains 65 common sight words to help young readers improve their reading fluency and comprehension. This book also teaches young readers several important content words. These words are paired with pictures to aid in learning and improve understanding.

Page	Sight Words First Appearance
4	every, is, on, year
5	a, day, find, how, it, last, long, out, to, will
7	after, America, animal, been, for, has, in, lives, named, that, the, under
8	be, comes, does, if, its, more, not, of, people, said, say, see, there
11	first, from, place, took
12	together
13	at
14	go, one, others, shown, some, was, watch, way
16	also
17	and, each, take
18	can, children, he, his, most, own
21	all, are

Page	Content Words First Appearance
4	February, Groundhog Day
5	winter
7	ground, hole
8	groundhog, shadow, spring, weeks
11	Candlemas, celebration, Germany, Pennsylvania, settlers, tradition
13	Gobbler's Knob, Punxsutawney
14	ceremony, New York City, television, Times Square
16	United States
17	events, Garner, Lincoln, Massachusetts, North Carolina
18	club, Punxsutawney Phil
21	activities, concerts, fireworks, tours

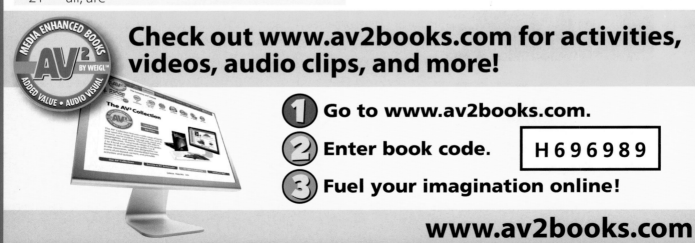